Musings From a Mess

We can do this, can't we?

Elizabeth Archer

BookLeaf Publishing

India | USA | UK

Dedication

To those who have ever stepped into a room and felt they were judged, who worry they are too much—come with me. This is for us.

Acknowledgments

I thank the group chat—Jess, Jess, and Lisa. I cannot describe the wondrous impact you three have had on my life. I have learned real love from you, and the patience and encouragement you all have given have helped lead me here.

To my mom and my ex for breaking me so completely that I had no choice but to rise as something new entirely—I won't thank you, but boy is the new me kicking ass.

To everyone at work who has listened to me gripe and has held me through it all, I cannot thank you enough. I always knew that where I landed would matter more than the job itself, and that has everything to do with the people you're with. You're all amazing.

To Lady, who reads my poems and knows me better than the rest of my friends—we've been through it, girl. And look at where we are.

To Steph, whom I have always admired and to whom I've secretly been jealous for decades, your unwavering love and support have meant so much.

To my dad—thank you for showing me that it's never too late to heal and start over.

I love you guys. Phew.

Preface

Some of these poems are deeply personal, and some are inspired by great poetry prompts. Regardless of where they came from or how they came about, I ascribe to the notion that once you consume them, they are yours.

Whatever meaning they hold for you is true. So take the ones that resonate and leave the rest.

Tricycle

My 3 wheels were not enough.

I remember.
Yes, I remember that day.
You were 5.
The rain, a steady drizzle, drenching me.
You came out of the house with a bag.
What it was full of, I never knew.
You walked fast and aimed straight for me.

You worked so hard to fit that bag on my
back step.
It was difficult. And you cried.
You gave up and held it instead.
As you sat down, a voice was at the back
door.

You yelled back, and I could not discern if
your tears or the rain fell harder.
"Away," you said. I'm going away

You pedaled valiantly...

But you carried too much. The load was
heavy.
You gave up.
Hauled the bag in.
I'm sorry my 3 wheels were not enough.

Ode To The Unsettled

Quiet.

That moment when you wake in the Spring to
open the window and breathe the crisp air
that sighs of dew and the gentle collapse of
night.

Quiet.

While speckled black is wrapped in the arms
of the morning, like a new mother folds her
own into a blanket and tucks away a tuft of
hair.

Quiet.

As birds tentatively chirp to coax the daffodil
and tiger lily out to play.

Quiet.

Like the fawn stumbling in a field after a lone
butterfly in the rays of the sun, while mist

whips through tall grass and rays of sun guide
them both.

Take it in.

The quiet.
The stillness of these moments.
Breathe them in and let them become the
very air within your lungs
and the beating of your drumming heart.
It is your song.

A Corpse Cannot Give

When I said, "That Hurt Me,"
You raised the gun and said, "What about
me?"
You always had it loaded
So why did you wait to pull the trigger until I
laid out my heart?
Until I peeled off my layers one by one so that
I could crack myself open and expose what
made me tick?
My heart beating in front of you for the
taking?
And you took
the shot.
Year 1—Bang
Year 2—Bang
Year 3 and 4 and 5…
BANG
You killed me 100 times.
Watched as I faltered and fell to my grave.
Then you looked down and asked me to pull
myself out and tell you
"I'm sorry."
BANG

Pull myself out.
"I love you."
BANG
Pull myself out.
"I'm here for you."
BANG
How many times did you think I'd have the
strength to keep coming back?
To climb over that ledge where you were
waiting, aiming the gun, just for you to say
"Why won't you talk?"
As if I could find breath after crawling.
As if I could find words while staring at a
smoking gun.
As if my heart still beat.
A corpse cannot give.

Me, Too

I have ruined many women—their lovers
hearing, "I'm sorry, I can't."

I am the missing leg on a chair, the bark lost
to a metal collar, the broken spine of a
favorite book.

I am found in water rushing under ice, in
headlights on a highway at night, in an
eyelash fallen off a thumb before it turned to
a wish.

My desire is destruction.
I am a gatherer of souls. Death's got nothing
on me.

I am an infection,
My voice growling in the vein—
"Don't forget me."
And you won't

Because I have become you.

Like lovers in a field of flowers, under a
solitary tree, carve into your skin a promise:
Rape.

The Pull

My blood is the sea.

Its tide pulls me back and forth, back and
forth.

Back and forth.

Never settled.

Endless, and I am bound.

It's a song I can't quite hear, though I'm
always listening.

If you wonder why my eyes glaze and my
body stills—

It is for the sea.

Careful, Now

They said something mean about me and
didn't notice it was mean.

Their words formed of charcoal, yet hung
suspended in the air and hid like shadows.

Ants crawled over their mouths, thick, like
asphalt, then stuck to me like wet coffee
grounds.

At midnight, their words fell like ash. My
body covered in soot I could not wipe off—

And they? They floated away on a sea of ink,
for they said something mean about me and
did not notice it was mean.

Loss

They try to bring comfort... "Everything
happens for a reason."

I try to guess what the reason is.

Perhaps, the reason is loneliness?

The house the tornado spared after it ruined
the rest.

Or maybe anger.

A red welt left from a hand no longer here.

Or—it's desperation.

A lone boat floated out too far, the saltwater
lapping at the edges denying refreshment.

Whatever the reason, they did not bring
comfort.

Because they had not experienced

What I had experienced.

"I Love You"—Dad

He didn't say I love you, but when I melodramatically raved about finally becoming a teenager at 13, he bought me a bouquet of roses.

He didn't say I love you, but he coached my T-Ball team.

He didn't say I love you, but when I mentioned saving for a radio attachment to play CDs in my car, it magically appeared already installed within days.

He didn't say I love you, but when my college boyfriend broke up with me just before Valentine's Day, he took me out so I wouldn't feel alone.

He didn't say I love you, but when I told him and mom that I was unexpectedly pregnant at 21, he watched me crumble as mom began weeping and walked out the door without a word, so he looked at me and said,

"Congratulations—You're glowing."

He didn't say I love you, but he did. Over and over he did.

Unintended Consequences

My brain enlisted, geared up for war. Put on armor that no longer fits.

My brain enlisted, but only after being recruited. By her. And by him.

It was not overnight, this outcome. And like most who join, my brain did not understand the severity or the length of time it would be fighting.

My brain enlisted, and that armor is so much worse than ill-fitting. It is an animal left to its own devices for too long.

It pinches me.
And bites me.

It squeezes and constricts me.

What once served a purpose is now only a cage.

I want free, but I've yet to win the battle.

I resent and regret the recruiters.

I must unlearn the battle cries and strategies, but my brain was a good soldier.

Just Admit It

"I can't live with another depressed person in this house"

"If I had a gun, I'd shoot myself"

"Your father never gave me flowers"

"Did you even brush your hair"

"I'd kill your dad if I could"

"What's on your face"

"No matter how you treated me, I still care about you"

"If there was a gun in this house, I'd use it"

"I'm too old to heal"

It would be nice if you would just admit that you don't like me

And that you wish I'd never been, because
then I'd be free

To not like you back

Yearning

I want it. That feeling when…

You're 16 in high school, and it's midnight. Your friends surround you, all sharing your deepest thoughts, and it hits you. You're suspended in a moment so sweet you're terrified for it to end because you know pure bliss and peace are fleeting.

You've just made eye contact with the one who clouds your vision and makes you smile —They touch your arm.

Blood surges…

Flies around in your veins, showing the excitement you don't dare allow on your face lest they find out you (LIKE) them.

You're sitting outside on the first truly warm day of Spring, feeling warmth cover you inch by inch, and you catch glimpses of red, yellow, and orange.

A book in your hand.
The buzzing of bees.
The chirping of birds in your ears.
You have all day to linger.

I yearn for more than moments.
To hold out my arms and gather to me those
fleeting feelings
And wrap them around me like a second skin.

Ode To Me

The truth is, I don't forgive myself.

But if I did—

It would be running water diving off a cliff, crashing with purpose and glee to collide below and become something else.

It would be the new skin grown after injury, tender and red and raw—but fresh and resilient.

It would be your first solo jump out of an airplane as the sun blinds you and the wind breaks upon your skin, and you settle into the fall just enough to yank the cord and snap up before the slow float to the ground.

The truth is—I don't forgive myself, but what a glorious freedom it will be when I do.

What Are You Waiting For?

You are the lightning and the thunder. A call, then a response. Look at me. HEAR ME.

You are the grass stubbornly thriving through cracks in concrete.

You are the phoenix, beautiful and triumphant in blazing orange and red, who becomes more than this world can handle, and so you erupt in order to appease, but you will not stay small. Oh no. There you go again, endlessly rising to heights others cannot even see.

You are a redwood standing tall and wide who will not be felled by something as trivial as lightning in a 100-year storm.

Do not fret. Do not fear.

You are the force to be weathered.

What are you waiting for?

The Key...

Was lost years ago underneath the dirt and worms—now full of flaky rust.

The garden it unlocks is full of blooms and noisy birds—vines that have laid claim to walls and trees whose roots reach under the gate, never to be contained.

The key has been used by others who know the trick of getting it into the lock.

I never learned its secret before it left me like Gollum's ring. I didn't know how precious it was until too late.

Once, I found another—tried in vain to make it fit, barely glimpsing the beauty and chaos within.

Trusting unknown benevolence,

I placed it on my key ring, hoping to find the way someday.

The weight in my pocket is enough comfort.

For now.

True Love

We've heard that love is quiet. Calm.

Yet it is anything but.

Real love is loud. And relentless.

It does not cower; it does not hide.

It makes itself known. And you do not have
to question.

Real love is a herd of elephants sounding the
alarm to gather together for one.

It is the needle buzzing into your skin to
mark you forever because it will never leave.

Real love is the river needling a canyon
through time, growing ever deeper.

Real love craves the chaos that life brings.

And through cursing and crying,

It helps you untangle.

Book

I could never have imagined I might
experience such joy.

I sat on a shelf for eons, overlooked by
thousands.

I was teased by hands that nearly stroked my
spine, but continued on to my neighbors.

But then, you.

You did not grab me. Rather, you gently
pulled me free.

You opened me, and I stretched my spine for
the first time.

You considered my words with a look so
intense, I did not know how to react.

You carried me under your arm,
gave me warmth.

Then—home. You consumed me in the best way. I did not mind when you wrote on my pages—it was a comforting caress.

You folded my corners, and it was a promise.

You would return.

And return you did.

You read me over and over. I got to see the sun with you and hear the steady patter of rain. Feel the sigh of a cat's tail as you cried and laughed over my contents.

Now, sitting on your shelf, I am not alone as I once was. I live amongst family who have felt the same joy.

What Could Have Been

I found you, hidden. A picture lost in time.

I could not fathom what I saw. The two of
you. Smiling. Genuine laughter so clear I
could hear its shimmer.

But it was foreign. And I was confused even
as I felt such joy.

I took in every detail.

The long hair: red.

Full beard to match.

Both gone long before my time.

The other—a near pixie cut and the brightest
smile I'd ever seen.

How?

The wrinkles in your face had yet to appear.

The sorrow and pain had not attached
themselves to your eyes.

I wondered about this version of you and
what role I may have played in morphing you
both to your current forms.

Would the joy have lasted?

I wept for these versions I did not know.

I wept for me; I wept for you.

Time gone by.

Unsent Letter

I wish everything had been different.

I wish I'd understood during what was happening.

I wish we'd never been.

I wish you knew the impact you've had.

I wish you knew my body rebels with chills and adrenaline each time we talk or see one another.

I wish you'd apologized and taken accountability.

I wish you didn't perceive my silence as infantile, but rather saw it for truth—

Fear of your reactions.

I wish I hadn't loved you so hard.

I wish I'd had more confidence.

I wish I had left you instead of the other way around.

I wish I'd chosen me, even once.

I wish I could believe you moving on has nothing to do with how little you loved me.

I wish you knew the despair that lives within me.

Because of you.

I regret every second.

It feels like a lie.

None of it was true.

I'm pretty sure—

I think I might hate you.

The Limelight

The moment is almost here.
I stand at the front.
Close my eyes and take a deep breath.
Then another.

They will be here soon. A sea of faces
To judge.
I hope I am enough.
That they take something away from my
performance.

I know that not all of them will.
There will be hecklers.
Interruptions.

I will ignore those I can.
And begrudgingly address those I must.

A look will be shared with a few. A dip of the
head in understanding.

I know it will never end in applause.

The most I can hope for are some smiles rather than groans.

I have accepted this.

A chime to indicate the start. Here they come. I open my eyes. Take a step forward:

"Good Morning, Class."

Someday

I will sit outside at a cafe in Greece wearing a beautifully simple, white dress. I will drink something sparkly and intoxicating as I half read a book and half people watch. There will be a breeze that ruffles my long brown hair just enough that I must adjust it every few minutes. At that moment, the waiter will bring me a refill, and his eyes will linger on me just long enough to convince me he's interested. A small smile grows as he walks away. When I finish my drink, I will take in the sights. Architecture and art. I will take it in slowly. All day.

I will wake up the next morning just before dawn and sit as my breath hitches at the sun glistening on the water and reflecting the homes on the hillside. Another long dress on my body, blowing with the breeze from the sea. I feel immaculate. I feel powerful. I feel unstoppable and joyous and free. I smile again, but bigger than before. And it doesn't leave my face

All day.

All week.

All the rest of my days.

I have found it. Me.

If We Only Knew

Remember when we were kids?

You would read an epic story or watch an
adventure in movies?

And when it was done, your chest swelled
with the enormous promise of glory?

Your very bones buzzed at the need to
conquer. To be the hero. To fall epically in
love.

And there was nobody and no experience you
knew to keep those from reality.

You went to the backyard and climbed the
jungle gym—mountain.

You jumped from the swing—plane.
You fought the tree—bad guy.

And you always won.

You swung your stick—sword and traversed
the stone pathway—river to the other side to
free your one true love.

We didn't know the hope would leave us.

That time and responsibilities and "Grown
Up" would take our fire.

But. It didn't have to.

Allow yourself to get it back.

Let's be kids—yeah?

* 9 7 8 9 3 6 9 5 4 3 6 7 0 *